An Anthology by Dr. Marilyn E. Porter

AFFIRMATIONS & ANTIDOTES THAT REMIND ME

Soulidified Publishing LLC™, Atlanta, Georgia
A Subsidiary of Pearly Gates Publishing LLC™

An Anthology by Dr. Marilyn E. Porter

AFFIRMATIONS & ANTIDOTES THAT REMIND ME

Copyright © 2017
Dr. Marilyn E. Porter

All Rights Reserved.
No portion of this publication may be reproduced, stored in any electronic system, or transmitted in any form or by any means (electronic, mechanical, photocopy, recording, or otherwise) without written permission from the publisher. Brief quotations may be used in literary reviews.

Unless otherwise stated, all Scripture passages are taken from the King James Version (KJV) of the Holy Bible.

ISBN 13: 978-1945117695
ISBN 10: 1945117699
Library of Congress Control Number: 2017940150

Published by:
Soulidified Publishing LLC™
A Christian Publisher located in Atlanta, Georgia (USA)

Affirmations & Antidotes That Remind Me

Dedication

Affirmations & Antidotes That Remind Me is dedicated to every person who has **never** taken the time to affirm who they are and have not come to know that they are *FEARFULLY-* and *WONDERFULLY-made* by an **ALMIGHTY CREATOR**.

An Anthology by Dr. Marilyn E. Porter

Acknowledgments

I will not name you all individually, but I truly want say *"Thank You"* to each of the authors who wrote on this project. It was such a smooth journey from start to finish!

Thank you to Pearly Gates Publishing LLC™ for functioning as the **BEST** editorial team ever!

Last (but NEVER least), to **GOD - MY GOD - BE ALL** of the glory and honor and praise!

~ Dr. Marilyn "M.E." Porter ~

Affirmations & Antidotes That Remind Me

About Your Compiler

Dr. Marilyn "M.E." Porter is affectionately regarded as The Soul Shifter™ by her clients, colleagues, and audiences. She is the Senior Pastor of "The Soul Restoration Center (SRC LIVE! - The Virtual Church Unusual)"™ and The Pink Pulpit Crusade International™. Dr. Porter is known for her easy-going truth-telling methods of ministry that is saturated in love. She is the CEO of The Soul INpowerment Group™ which houses Soulidified Publishing LLC™ and where she serves as both a Spiritual Life and Personal Development Coach, as well as Business Adviser.

Dr. Porter is a powerful motivational and transformational speaker who tackles issues such as self-worth, soul healing, and becoming your unflappable self. All topics developed come right out of the pages of her own life's story. In her Amazon Best-Selling autobiographical journal, *The Pieces of ME (And YOU)*, Dr. Porter reveals many of those experiences, to include: childhood rape, abortion, and divorce.

At a young age, she peeked her head into the world of entrepreneurship, but without proper guidance and complete knowledge, she didn't know where to begin. All of that changed with the wonderful world of social media! In 2012, she began her journey as a Life Coach through serving others from a Facebook page she titled "Motivationally ME". From there, she became a well-known and highly sought-after Spiritual Life Coach - which didn't take long to spiral into her becoming known as a phenomenal Business Adviser, Speaker Developer, and Writing Coach - which she simply refers to as "Personal Development".

An Anthology by Dr. Marilyn E. Porter

Whether from the pulpit or the main stage, Dr. Porter captivates the hearts of her listeners because it is from her own heart that she speaks. It is her love of people - a respect for God's beloved creations - that M.E. goes above and beyond the call of duty to speak life, write life, preach life, coach life, and live a life that honors the gifts, talents, and anointing on her own life to heal through the power of words.

Dr. Porter is famously known for the following statement:

"I am Unflappable - because if you stop my physical body, my SOUL will not be moved!"

Dr. Porter is poised to reach the entire globe with the positive message of Christ's love using every possible modality. As a lover of music, there is an inspirational music project in her foreseeable future - an accomplishment her three daughters are sure to join in on!

To learn more about Dr. Porter visit her website:
www.marilyneporter.com

Book Dr. Porter for speaking engagements or coaching:
info@marilyneporter.com

Affirmations & Antidotes That Remind Me

Foreword

Dr. Marilyn Porter knows and understands the power of words - and she affirms this with the release of *Affirmations & Antidotes That Remind Me*. She is a woman who has lived a life filled with adversity, yet through the power of her words - her own confessions - she has triumphed!

I have listened to Dr. Porter encourage and empower others in such a way that one can see the very life come back into their eyes. She is certainly someone who is qualified to gather others to bring this project to life. I am honored to have my own words fill space in this book.

I have seen the manifestation of Dr. Porter's positive words. I understand that she does more than just speak positivity; she speaks The Word of God in her own tone in a way that others can soak up God's glory, even when they don't realize it.

This very book is a result of the power of affirming words spoken by a woman who believes what she speaks. Do you believe your own words? If so, what are you speaking? I would like to offer you this advice: Take this book, read it, meditate on it, and begin to form your own affirmations for life. OH! And don't forget the antidotes…the life solutions!

~ Dr. Walter Sims ~
The Minister of Motivation

TABLE OF CONTENTS

DEDICATION -- VI

ACKNOWLEDGMENTS -- VII

ABOUT YOUR COMPILER --- VIII

FOREWORD -- X

DONNA HICKS IZZARD --- 1

ERAINA TINNIN -- 5

KALI S. STEWARD --- 9

ALISON FELICIANO -- 13

CRYSTAL KIA-PAUL -- 17

PASTOR JEFFREY MOORE --- 21

KENDAL WILLIAMS -- 23

LAKELL MAXWELL -- 27

NAOMI SMITH TEJADA -- 33

PASTOR MAGGY REED -- 35

SHARLRITA DELOATCH -- 41

MINISTER ALMENA MAYES -- 43

STEPHANIE STANFORD -- 49

STEVII AISHA MILLS -- 51

TIESHA C. FRONTIS --- 53

TOYA HAMLETT --- 57

ANDRENA PHILLIPS -- 61

YOLANDA CHEATHAM	65
ONIKA SHIRLEY	69
FELICIA LUCAS	71
NOTES TO SELF	75
CONTACT DR. MARILYN E. PORTER	91
OTHER M.E. PORTER TITLES	92

An Anthology by Dr. Marilyn E. Porter

DONNA HICKS IZZARD

Donna Hicks Izzard is a Best-Selling Author, Speaker, and Minister. Donna is best known as the "Parellelpreneur and Identity Strategist". Her work centers on giving individuals the tools they need to move forward in all aspects of their lives, including personal, business, and ministry.

Donna is a featured contributor in the "I AM AMERICA" Cookbook, along with Chef Jeff and Tavis Smiley.

Donna, along with former "White House Ambassador" Susan D. Johnson Cook as her Business Manager, has been the driving force behind the development of the prestigious Hampton Minister's Conference that hosts over 10,000 ministers annually.

In her professional career, Donna is one of the few women to serve as a Technology-Training Executive at a top-level law firm.

Affirmations & Antidotes That Remind Me

DONNA'S AFFIRMATION:

I WAS CREATED BY THE CREATOR TO BE CREATIVE.

God created you in...
"*So, God created man in His own image; in the image of God He created him; male and female He created them*" (Genesis 1:27, NKJV).

God filled you in...
"*And the Lord God formed man of the dust of the ground, and breathed into his nostrils the breath of life; and man became a living being*" (Genesis 2:7, NKJV).

God gave you purpose in...
"*But to each one of us grace was given according to the measure of Christ's gift*" (Ephesians 4:7, NKJV).

REMINDS ME THAT:

When I state this affirmation, I am reminded of who I am so that when I am 'playing small' or not operating in the creative gifts I was created for, I am convicted.

An Anthology by Dr. Marilyn E. Porter

DONNA'S ANTIDOTE

Embracing your creativity is more than looking and feeling good; it's about knowing who the Masterful Creator is. It's about intentionally operating in your Creative Gifts. It relates to self-image and self-esteem. It determines how a person views himself or herself in relation to other people.

God formed you in Genesis 1:27, filled you in Genesis 2:7, and in Ephesians 4:7, He supplied the purpose.

Our God is the Masterful Creator - the source of **ALL** creativity. He gave us gifts of creativity when He created us in His image. Although we are not all created with the same creative gifts, we all have creative gifts inside of us.

God - in His wisdom - gave us the creative gifts that make us who we are. We honor Him by utilizing and developing the gifts He deposited inside of us. It is not our place to question God on the type of creative gifts He gave us.

I often hear many people state, "*You are so creative*" or "*I am not as creative as you*". That is the furthest thing from the truth. For example, whenever you start a task or a project, solve a problem, or create something from your mind, it's all a part of creativity! Being 'creative' has many forms. We all use our creative gifts differently. What one person sees as creative, another may not. Creativity is in the eye of the beholder. No one can tell you what a creative gift is and what it is not. Our grace and purpose are aligned with the creative gifts God has deposited in you.

For example, I was often told things such as:
"*You're doing too much.*"
"*You are so creative! What can't you do?*"
"*You have too many things you're involved in.*"

Affirmations & Antidotes That Remind Me

All of these statements related to me operating in my creative gifts - and I was made to feel guilty about them...*OFTEN*. One particular instance stands out for me, and it was when I had just begun my journey as a Minister. A Pastor told me I would have to put away my creative passions and concentrate on ministry. I was crushed, but took the Pastor's comments very seriously and started shutting down areas where I was serving in my creative gifts. That was until the day I heard the voice of the Lord clearly tell me, *"I created you and gave you those gifts for My glory!"*

It was at that very moment I realized:

I WAS CREATED BY THE CREATOR TO BE CREATIVE!

I then understood my 'why'. I started back serving and operating in my gifts to honor God. I teach everyone that they were creatively created to be creative. It is our responsibility as heirs to honor, embrace, and thank God for our creative gifts - as well as to use and develop our creative gifts for His glory!

Are **YOU** fully operating in **YOUR** creative gifts?

An Anthology by Dr. Marilyn E. Porter

ERAINA TINNIN

Eraina Tinnin is a Speaker (affectionately called an 'Inspirational Powerhouse'), professional Life Coach, and entrepreneur. She has been named an "Encourager" because of her unfailing ability to lift the spirits of others.

She is a contributing writer with *Authentically You Magazine*, International Best-Selling Author of *Becoming a Beautiful You*, and co-author of *Healing Toxic Habits* (to be released April 2017).

Eraina is the Founder of an online ministry called "Sistahs in Spirit". She has a Master's Degree in Human Services with a specialization in Marriage & Family Therapy from Liberty University. She is a wife and mother.

Affirmations & Antidotes That Remind Me

ERAINA'S AFFIRMATION

I AM AN ORIGINAL; NOT A CARBON COPY. THERE IS NO ONE ELSE IN THE ENTIRE WORLD LIKE ME. I AM A MASTERPIECE WHO WAS UNIQUELY CREATED. I AM AN INDIVIDUAL WHO IS SET APART FROM THE REST. NO ONE CAN DO WHAT I CAN DO. GOD CREATED ME JUST THE WAY I AM - FLAWS AND ALL. I AM NOT A MISTAKE. I AM NOT AN ACCIDENT. I AM HERE FOR A REASON AND A PURPOSE. THE ADVERSITIES I HAVE OVERCOME, THE TRIALS, TRIBULATIONS, OBSTACLES, AND CHALLENGES ALL MADE ME WHO I AM. THE WAY I WALK AND TALK IS LIKE NONE OTHER. I AM SPECIAL. I AM SET APART.

So, why don't I feel that way? Why are there things I don't like about myself? Why are there things I try to change in an effort to make it better? The choices I've made may not have been the best - and that's okay! I live and I learn. My choices are not a reason to be down on myself, but should encourage me to make wiser choices in the future. If I am not where I want to be in life, instead of complaining, I should do something to change my circumstances. There may be others who resemble me and have characteristics like me, but there is **NO ONE** in the entire universe **JUST LIKE ME**.

REMINDS ME THAT:

God says in His Word that I am fearfully and wonderfully made. I am more than a conqueror. I am the head and not the tail. I am also reminded that I can do all things through Christ who gives me strength. I am so special, He knows the number of hairs on my head! I am a peculiar person, a royal priesthood who stands apart. I am reminded that I am chosen. I am a child of the King!

An Anthology by Dr. Marilyn E. Porter

ERAINA'S ANTIDOTE

I must not compare myself with others' successes, their lives, and their accomplishments. I must constantly seek ye first the Kingdom of God and all of His righteousness. I must keep in mind that what God has for me is for me. Just like I am uniquely 'me', so are the things that God has for me. I must never forget that I am His. If God is for me, who can be against me?

The remedy is to fill myself up with God's Word so that when negative thoughts come my way, His Word is what comes out. I am so full of Christ, that is who people see when they see me. I allow my light to shine in the good and the bad, knowing that God has my back and will never forsake me.

Affirmations & Antidotes That Remind Me

An Anthology by Dr. Marilyn E. Porter

KALI S. STEWARD

Kali S. Steward is a native of New York who currently resides in Massachusetts. She is an Author, Writer, Entrepreneur, and Owner of EHCS. Kali is a Blogger, assisting with content for many businesses. Her mantra is, "Networking with women is very important because women do it differently". She believes by utilizing our circle to inspire each other, we leave a lasting impression in each other's lives.

She is also an advocate for children, with a passion for utilizing her time to help those in the system by offering them hope while in transition. She also operates a health care business.

Kali's book projects include: *Affirmation & Antidotes That Remind Me*, *Beauty of Color Collection*, and Amazon Best-Selling *C&D for the Woman's Soul* and *Majesty of Motherhood*.

Affirmations & Antidotes That Remind Me

KALI'S AFFIRMATION

MY STRENGTH IS KNOWING THAT IN THIS JOURNEY, I'M NOT ALONE. GOD HAS NOT FORSAKEN ME, BUT HAS RESTORED ME WHEN THE ECHOES OF MY VOICE THAT WERE ONCE SILENCED BEGAN TO SHATTER DURING THOSE DAUNTING MOMENTS OF CAPTIVITY OF MY OWN SELF-EXPRESSION ON HOW I VIEWED THE WORLD...NOT WHAT OTHERS EXPECTED ME TO BE.

"For God has not given us the spirit of fear and timidity, but of power, love, and self-discipline" (2 Timothy 1:7, NLT).

REMINDS ME THAT:

In my early years of adulthood, one day a light of hope touched my heart. It was the awakening of a new world in a circumference of a bubble being rebirthed from my mother's womb...a new existence of my spirit being connected to something greater than me.

Oftentimes, I've asked God to give me peace in my valley of uncertainty. He assured me - His daughter - that He was with me at the moment of my conception and He was with me now. As life continuously revolves, failures are the roadblocks that lead us towards our destination of truth and the knowledge to realize that all things unforeseen are the attributes of what is coming.

An Anthology by Dr. Marilyn E. Porter

KALI'S ANTIDOTE

The Spring of 2013, Easter Sunday in Freeport, New York at Perfecting Faith Church was a moment that forever changed my life. It was as if the second row from the pulpit (with only one seat left) was waiting for me. The sermon that Sunday was on Women Preachers. I could feel the anointing of the sisters from the left to the right and from the front to the back as they consoled me in the comfort of God's hands protecting me.

That day, Pastor Donnie McClurkin preached about how back in Bible days, women were preachers way before it was acceptable in congregations. Women were not only devoted, but had faith that better days would come - just as Mary Magdalene believed as she stood outside of Jesus' tomb in tears (John 20:11-13). As she wept, she bent over to look into the tomb and saw two angels in white seated where Jesus' body had been: one at the head and the other at the foot. They asked her, "Woman, why are you crying?"

That very moment, I could not stop crying. My faith had been tested at every turn. Even when the people closest to me let me down, I knew I could depend on Jesus. As the manifestation of the glory of God spoke through a woman at the altar near me, she whispered in my ear and prayed over me. She spoke of things that only God would know...things I never told anyone.

You see, it was very easy for me to adapt to my environment, camouflaged like a chameleon where no one could 'see' me. However, how could I fulfill God's destiny He had for me? I was not ready for what He already told me I would be so long ago because of my own fear.

Affirmations & Antidotes That Remind Me

Feeling the peace in my valley freed me from bondage. All of those things that had held me back and kept me from stepping into my purpose were falling away. All I could do was praise God in the midst of it all.

"I've wiped away your transgressions like a cloud and your sins like mist. Return to me; because I've redeemed you" (Isaiah 44:22).

I will carry those words with me forever.

An Anthology by Dr. Marilyn E. Porter

ALISON FELICIANO

Alison Feliciano is a C.E.O., Speaker, Author, and Credit & Debt Coach. Most importantly, she is the mother of two children which are her priority. She calls it the *Inner Circle*. Alison says, *"If you protect and teach the Inner Circle, outside of it you are Unstoppable!"*

Alison has been in the finance, mortgage, and real estate industries in different capacities for almost 27 years. She has been published in four books and will have several personal projects coming out soon. Although she is passionate about educating people in areas of Credit and Debt, above all else, it's her calling to help people to Dream Big!

Affirmations & Antidotes That Remind Me

AFFIRM *OTHERS!*

Do you know how many people have never been told, "You are a winner"? There are most likely people in your life right now - people you work with, play ball with, maybe even your own family members - who are starving for your approval. They are craving for you to speak the blessing over their life.

You don't know what it will mean to them to be affirmed by you just by giving them your approval and let them know (in no uncertain terms) that you are proud of them and believe they will do great things. Everyone wants and needs to be valued. Everyone needs to be appreciated. Every person needs that blessing.

Let me ask you this: What kinds of seeds are you planting in your child, your spouse, 'that' friend, niece, or nephew? Are you believing in anyone? Are you taking an interest to see how you can make someone's life better? Listen to their dreams. Find out what God has put in their hearts. Let them know you're behind them. Give them your approval.

If you talk with any successful people, they will tell you somebody believed in them. Somebody planted a seed and encouraged them when they were down. Somebody helped them get a good break. Somebody spoke faith when they didn't think they could do it.

Thomas Edison encouraged Henry Ford. Mr. Ford was introduced to him as "the man trying to build a car that runs on gasoline". When Edison heard it, his face brightened up. He hit his fist on the table and said, "You've got it! A car that has its own power plant. That's a brilliant idea!"

An Anthology by Dr. Marilyn E. Porter

Up to that point, no one had encouraged Mr. Ford. No one thought it was a good idea. He had just about convinced himself to give up, but along came Edison and spoke faith into him. That was the turning point in Henry Ford's life. He said, "I thought I had a good idea, but I started to doubt myself. Then, along came one of the greatest minds that has ever lived and gave me his complete approval!"

That's what can happen with a simple vote of confidence. We don't realize the power we hold. We don't always realize what it means when we tell somebody, "I believe in you. You have what it takes. I'm behind you 100%!" Each and every single one of us should be another's #1 Fan. We should be encouraging them, lifting them when they've fallen, celebrating them when they succeed, praying for them when they're struggling, and urging them forward.

That's what is means to be a "People-Builder".

Affirmations & Antidotes That Remind Me

An Anthology by Dr. Marilyn E. Porter

CRYSTAL KIA-PAUL

Crystal Kia-Paul is a Motivational Spiritual Teacher, Healer, and Certified Life Coach. She learned early on to help others by the example her parents set. Crystal loves to share and teach Oneness through the richness of her Hawaiian culture. Her primary focus is helping people resolve inner conflicts by having them reconnect to Ke Akua *(Hawaiian for God)* and remembering their innate gifts of Aloha *(Love)*, Malu *(Peace)*, Le'a *(Joy)*, and 'Ike *(Wisdom)*.

Crystal is married to Ron Paul, the man of her dreams and business partner for over 25 years.

They currently reside in north Texas with their furbaby zoo.

Affirmations & Antidotes That Remind Me

AFFIRMATION: I WILL EMBRACE SOLITUDE

A friend recently became single after a 10+ year relationship. Some of the greatest fears had been realized; being alone and doing things alone.

Does this sound familiar? Do you know someone who harnesses those traits? I'm talking about that person who always has to have someone - a significant other - in his or her life. We come into this world alone, and we leave alone - yet we are not meant to be alone; we are meant to have someone with us.

Talk about contradictions!

Is there a difference in being alone, being lonely, or embracing solitude? Yes, there is! The difference is in the choice you make. You can choose to be alone, alienating others in your social group (i.e. family, friends, or co-workers). However, you can be lonely in a crowd of thousands for a variety of reasons. Having the strength to embrace solitude is an innate gift you have.

Embracing solitude is the strength of faith and belief in Ke Akua *(Hawaiian for God, Creator, Source)*. Ancient Hawaiians lived a communal lifestyle by learning to live in harmony with their environment and everyone in their village. Conflicts amongst one another were handled by the Kupuna (Elder) of the family or the Kahuna (Master Spiritual Teacher) of the village - depending on the type of conflict. They knew that to solve any conflict or turmoil, a person had to go within for the answers.

An Anthology by Dr. Marilyn E. Porter

Many of us choose to look outside of ourselves for the answers. In a western society, we have been programmed to believe it's bad or shameful to be alone or in solitude. This is one of your greatest opportunities for the deepest connection and clarity to Ke Akua.

Simple Steps to Embrace the Solitude with Serenity, Vigor, and the Deepest Knowing of Ke Akua and Self.

1. Daily meditation is prayers. When we pray, we are asking of Ke Akua. When we meditate, we are listening for the answers from Ke Akua. Do both...together!
Morning Gratitude Meditation: Set your alarm clock for five minutes earlier than normal. Yes: Five minutes is all you need! Do this meditation before you get out of bed. Set your intentions for your day. Look at the world with childlike amazement.

2. *"I AM"* are the two most powerful words that describe how you communicate about **YOURSELF** and **KE AKUA**. Write out the following statements and place them next to the bathroom mirror:
    I AM LOVE. I AM PEACE. I AM JOY. I AM WISDOM.
While getting yourself together, read them as you are looking at JOYOUS SELF in the mirror.

3. Take a five-minute 'Daydream Break' while working. Imagine a recess time for you to play. You are a magnificent Co-Creator; allow yourself to create with Ke Akua!

4. Bedtime Meditation from Dr. Wayne Dyer: Don't allow yourself to think of the day's happenings. Instead, think of five things you are grateful for. When you do, allow your brain to marinate in 5 - 8 hours of infinite possibilities in gratitude.

Affirmations & Antidotes That Remind Me

When you know "Self" and what you can Co-Create with Ke Akua, you will appreciate and *CRAVE* the *SOLITUDE*.

An Anthology by Dr. Marilyn E. Porter

PASTOR JEFFREY MOORE

Pastor Jeffrey S. Moore is the founder of Healing Keys Ministry. The purpose of Healing Keys is to reach those who have experienced life challenges and, through his own experience and study of the Word of God, help them heal and find their God-ordained destiny. Jeffrey partners with other ministries, business owners, and entrepreneurs to ensure he reaches the maximum amount of people for the Kingdom. Healing Keys Ministry has numerous outreach ministries within its ministry including, Praise Orlando Radio Network, The Praise Network Global Radio, and Praise Orlando TV.

For more information about Jeffrey and Healing Keys Ministry go to www.helaingkeysministry.com

Affirmations & Antidotes That Remind Me

AFFIRMATION: IT'S IN ME!

"The word of the Lord came to me, saying, "Before I formed you in the womb I knew you, before you were born I set you apart; I appointed you as a prophet to the nations" (Jeremiah 1:4-5, NIV).

REMIINDS ME THAT:

This scripture has been my driving scripture for many seasons. When I first set out on my walk with God, I read this scripture - and everything that happened in my past made sense. As I continued my journey, God released me and elevated me. The scripture changed meanings, but the root meaning still held true.

I have found that whatever I am going through or what stands before me, I turn to this scripture and God reminds me that the power to reach my full potential is already in me - and has been before God formed me in the womb!

There is no reason you nor I can't go forward boldly with whatever task we have because God already knew us and set you and I apart from others.

An Anthology by Dr. Marilyn E. Porter

KENDAL WILLIAMS

Kendal Williams is a real-life Sex and Relationship Educator, Abundance Coach, Author, mother of seven, and lover of life. She is known for her raw, authentic, passionate style in teaching and coaching. She has co-authored books with David Riklin, Dr. Joseph Cilea, Dr. Joseph Mercola, Gary Craig, Dr. Marcus Laux, Dr. Susan Lark, Dr. Stephen Sinatra, Dr. Julian Whitaker, and Steven E. Kendal.

Kendal believes our sexuality is one of the greatest untapped areas of life and source of a deeper connection and healing to our authentic selves and the Creator.

You can explore her coaching and connect to her at **tantrictransformation@gmail.com** or **www.kendalwilliams.com** or **www.tantrictransformation.com**

Affirmations & Antidotes That Remind Me

AFFIRMATION:

THE DEEPER MY SURRENDER TO SELF, THE MORE AUTHENTIC MY VULNERABILITY WITH ALL OF LIFE. IN THIS VULNERABILITY, I FIND MY POWER AND I EMBRACE THE GOD-LIGHT WITHIN. IN THIS SPACE, I MANIFEST MY DESIRED LIFE.

REMINDS ME THAT:

Vulnerability breeds deep love and connection. It also carries with it our deepest insecurities, forcing us to experience and deal with our internal "crazy", which puts the spotlight on all of our fears. As we stand in our vulnerability and surrender deeper, we can breathe into this fear and come through it to a space of merging with our desires and dreams. It is in this true state of surrender that we connect to our authentic self.

An Anthology by Dr. Marilyn E. Porter

KENDAL'S ANTIDOTE

The more we lean into allowing our truth to lead, we open to physical, emotional, and spiritual vulnerability. From this space, we tap into our purpose. It is through this full surrender to self that we meet and align to the Creator within. Once embraced, our ONLY step to create the life that we desire is to ASK; ASK with certainty, clarity of intent, and joy in our heart.

Affirmations & Antidotes That Remind Me

An Anthology by Dr. Marilyn E. Porter

LAKELL MAXWELL

Lakell Maxwell is the Co-Creator and Journey Guide at LivingAsLakell.com. She is influential to the people she meets on a daily basis and in all facets of her life. She is a survivor of child molestation and knows how to turn life's lessons into teachable moments through the power of writing. Lakell is a volunteer at heart for charities such as Big Brother, Big Sister, The Hosea Williams Feed the Hungry, Soles 4 Souls, and CASA. She also has spoken to groups such as Ladies of Favor and Celebrate Recovery about molestation. She is a writer, singer (an alto, to be exact), and a peanut butter lover.

Affirmations & Antidotes That Remind Me

AFFIRMATION:
MY TODAY IS A RESULT OF MY YESTERDAY.

REMINDS ME THAT:
This reminds me that the actions I took yesterday will set me up for a better today.

LAKELL'S ANTIDOTE:
Sometimes, we remain stuck in the worries of yesterday instead of living in that day's "today" while we have a chance.

******

AFFIRMATION:
MY TRUTH BREATHES LIFE.

REMINDS ME THAT:
This reminds me to live my truth daily by speaking and teaching: LIVE AUTHENTICALLY!

LAKELL'S ANTIDOTE:
This life is full of lessons with buried truths. It is up to you to breathe life into them.

******

AFFIRMATION:
MY SCARS ARE THE STORY OF MY GREATNESS.

REMINDS ME THAT:
This reminds me to learn from the past, live in the present, and tell the story of my new future.

LAKELL'S ANTIDOTE:
I am a survivor of molestation who lives in my scars to uncover my greatness. I know my story will tell me the truth each and every time I need an answer to my next question.

An Anthology by Dr. Marilyn E. Porter

AFFIRMATION:
I AM INTUITIVELY AWAKE TO DECIDE MY NEXT 'YES'.

REMINDS ME THAT:
This reminds me to trust my intuition and to only make healthy decisions in order to stay soundly awake.

LAKELL'S ANTIDOTE:
I am learning to trust my decisions - which are God's decisions - to a blessed "yes".

******

AFFIRMATION:
I AM RESPONSIVE TO GOD'S TEMPLE.

REMINDS ME THAT:
This reminds me that to eat to live is to show God appreciation for my body's life.

LAKELL'S ANTIDOTE:
I am in constant struggle with my body and mind. I know that in order to honor HIM, I must honor myself and the trust HE has for me to take care of HIS temple.

******

AFFIRMATION:
I AM EMOTIONALLY OK TO FEEL.

REMINDS ME THAT:
This reminds me to check in with my emotions daily and know it is ok to feel. This is what makes me alive.

LAKELL'S ANTIDOTE:
When I check in, I check out what is really causing the current feeling and deciding to act on it *only* if it is a healthy choice. When I know the difference, I feel the difference.

Affirmations & Antidotes That Remind Me

AFFIMATION:
STAYING ALIVE IS TO SET BOUNDARIES.

REMINDS ME THAT:
This reminds me to set limits around myself to keep unwarranted opinions away from my calling.

LAKELL'S ANTIDOTE:
I learned later in life that boundaries keep me and my sanity in check and gives the person notice that I respect myself. The lack of boundaries shows a lack of self-control within.

******

AFFIRMATION:
I AM COMMITTED TO MY NOW.

REMINDS ME THAT:
This reminds me to turn off the busyness of the world in order to live in the moment now.

LAKELL'S ANTIDOTE:
This life is too short to not commit to what's going on around you right now. Today is your day to say "NO" without apology and "YES" with confidence. Own your day, and your NOW will keep you smiling.

******

An Anthology by Dr. Marilyn E. Porter

AFFIRMATION:
TO LOVE YOU IS TO BE IN UNCONDITIONAL LOVE WITH MYSELF.

REMINDS ME THAT:
This reminds me to continue to love me first in order to show my best to you.

LAKELL'S ANTIDOTE:
It took me 22 years to feel love again in order to know that I need to give that feeling to myself daily. I've lived with a mother who loved her relationships more than me. I've lived with a father who loved me, but decided to beat down my mother to show his love to her. I've lived with a stepfather who showed me his love by kissing the little me on the lips. I've learned in my previous life that love hurts and it abandons. I now know that love is unconditionally given only when I love the whole me.

******

AFFIRMATION:
I AM IN CONTROL OF MYSELF.

REMINDS ME THAT:
This reminds me that I decide my wants and desires. It's up to me if they live.

LAKELL'S ANTIDOTE:
I have learned that the lack of self-control is a direct reflection of how I show myself I am worthy. I must keep pushing towards my heart's desire each and every day.

******

Affirmations & Antidotes That Remind Me

AFFIRMATION:
I AM WORTH THE PROMISE.

REMINDS ME THAT:
This reminds me to fulfill every promise to myself, for this is how I honor my journey.

LAKELL'S ANTIDOTE:
I am alive and a work in progress. My journey is guided towards a greater me. YOUR journey is guided towards a greater you. Stay alive in it.

An Anthology by Dr. Marilyn E. Porter
NAOMI SMITH TEJADA

Naomi Smith Tejada is the Intercessory Prayer Warrior for Dr. Marilyn Porter. As many know, I have overcome many adversities in life. I raised three successful adult children on my own due to the untimely death of their father. I continued to struggle throughout life…BUT GOD! In putting God first, all things are possible.

Today, I aspire to open a small Bed and Breakfast beach resort for men and women in ministry to rejuvenate, along with a small café.

I am honored to be a part of this collaboration because indeed, there are times when we all need to be reminded of who we are in Christ.

Affirmations & Antidotes That Remind Me

AFFIRMATION:
MY MIND IS CLUTTER-FREE!

I want you to think of a time when you felt like your best wasn't good enough. Make a list of logistical, circumstantial, and spiritual truths that relate to your situation.

Look at your list, ask God to help you keep (or get) your mind clear of condemnation clutter the enemy has piled on your thoughts. Stand firm on God's truths and remain alert to the enemy's ploys. Using God's truth, keep making truth-filled assessments and wisdom-based adjustments with the Word of God.

"Be alert and of sober mind. Your enemy the devil prowls around like a roaring lion looking for someone to devour. Resist him, standing firm in the faith, because you know that the family of believers throughout the world is undergoing the same kind of sufferings" (1 Peter 5:8-9).

REMINDS ME THAT:

This Bible verse reminds me that it doesn't matter what choices I have made or the circumstances that I live in. God loves me and He thinks I am more than enough. His plans are so much better than anything I can ever fathom.

"For I know the plans I have for you," declares the Lord, "plans to prosper you and not to harm you, plans to give you hope and a future" (Jeremiah 19:11).

Thank you, Lord, for loving me - even when I did not love nor think much of myself. Father, I honor You, I praise You, and give You all the glory!

Amen.

An Anthology by Dr. Marilyn E. Porter

PASTOR MAGGY REED

Pastor Maggy Reed is an Ordained Pastor, Author, Publisher, Medical Inventor/Innovator, Multilingual Speaker, Clergy & Life Coach, Social Entrepreneur, and Humanitarian. She is a lover of life and arts. Her motto is, *"I'm here to enhance, empower, and inspire others to break through barricades in their life to finally tap into their calling; teaching how to break through it, write it, wear it, and speak it."*

Pastor Reed is the Chief Executive Officer of the following organizations: The Clergy Spot, Inc., Equipping Spiritual Leaders, Inc., and Inscribeit Publishing. She owns the patent for Mammelle Breast Pads™ and is the Founder of KaribAmerica's Well-Being Foundation, Inc.

Pastor Reed reminds each of us that no matter what God gave you in your life, with faith, confidence, determination and action, **nothing** will be impossible for you with God on your side.

Affirmations & Antidotes That Remind Me

AFFIRMATION:
I AM NEVER ALONE.

REMINDS ME THAT:

This reminds me that God will never leave me alone, abandon me, nor forsake me.

MAGGY'S ANTIDOTE:

From a very young age, I found myself constantly talking to God, usually in writing and arts. It was my 'normal'. I had no siblings to play with or talk to on a regular basis. I was always drawing pictures of dresses, peaceful beach views, trees, the beach, flowers, happy faces, heart shapes, or playing with a small sewing machine I owned. This was where I met the 'Prince of Peace'.

I had no idea the arts would play such a major role in my life, as well as those of the clients I am serving today.

I am grateful for God's reassurance to me growing up. Arts and prayers were my healing spot…a place where I felt loved. I was constantly looking for something that I had no real idea about. I only had a feeling, and I believed it. I was looking for someone to help me with answers to the many questions I had. The older I got, the harder it was. It became obvious that I was not going to get any of those answers. For some strange reason, I felt isolated, ashamed, abandoned, and pushed aside. I had all kinds of negative feelings going through my head - and no idea how to process them.

An Anthology by Dr. Marilyn E. Porter

I want to take a minute to speak to mothers at this time: Your children need reassurance from you. The adversary is after your child's mind, but your love, prayers, open communication, hugs, and understanding will be their healing balm from Gilead. It will be a dosage to keep your child at peace.

The older I got, the harder it became for me to understand what was happening to me, yet I had all of my basic needs met to make me a happy child. On the outside, it appeared I had it all; however, on the inside, I felt out of place, lost, and like I did not 'belong'. I needed to tell someone about my dreams to be a singer, dancer, pianist, and guitar player. I was longing for something…or someone.

One day, I went to buy a bag of cookies from the corner store. The woman there told me something I never heard of, yet it got me curious enough to go home and ask my mom what she meant. I did not get an answer - almost as if the conversation with that woman never happened. I was heartbroken.

I lived a very sheltered life in a Christian family with no other children, so I was constantly at church with my mom. Therefore, praying became the main 'thing' I did in my life. I was sad and lonely most of my life. I wanted to talk about a sister or brother, but no one knew that.

It shows in my photo here that I rarely smile.

A lady came to my house one day and started talking with my mom while I was washing my uniform for school. The word I had been looking for slipped out of her mouth accidentally, and she confirmed it - FINALLY! The truth came out. I was only 12 years old at the time. What I felt deep on the inside was real. The mystery was partially solved…

Affirmations & Antidotes That Remind Me

As a child, I was teased a lot by peers for being skinny. I did not get the reassurance I needed to hear. I never heard I was beautiful. I never received compliments. I lived a very boring childhood. I don't recall a meaningful event, something phenomenal to remember, nor a deep conversation. My parents gave me the order to keep away from playing with other children at school. I still could not understand why. We lived in a house that was gates, so no one could come in. I had to play behind the gate.

Back to the mystery...

I now know why no one ever told me the story of my birth. I now know why I never felt the love that other children talked about at school. I now know why no one ever said I looked like my mom or dad. I now know why I don't have a brother or sister. I now know the 'why' behind the avoidance I felt all of those years.

Imagine how lonely my life was. I lived in fear most of my life. I was always walking on eggshells in fear of disappointing my parents. That's why I was never disciplined with a belt...NEVER. I looked for answers everywhere to find out the source of that emptiness. To this day, no one can tell me where my family is on this planet Earth. The thought of this alone is scary for a child.

I could not live like that anymore. I released that endless pain to God because it affected my relationships as an adult. I was (admittedly) fearful of people abandoning me, so I clung on to unhealthy relationships.

An Anthology by Dr. Marilyn E. Porter

I started taking classes and prayed to God for Him to put people on my path who could help me with my struggles. Afraid of people hurting me, I kept to myself in an effort to protect my heart. I started praying for my heart and for deliverance from the sadness. As a result, my heart became very tender towards families. I started praying for hurting families, mentoring young adults on how to appreciate their parents - but no one knew why.

It goes way back to when I desired to start an orphanage in 2010. I started praying for forgiveness and experienced it in 2012. I continued to cultivate it every day. I was serious about my deliverance from resentments and holding grudges. I finally found my break in 2014 when I decided I must break through barricades in my life to succeed in my gifts, skills, talents, and anointing.

To be effective in my prayer life, I had to find the verses pertaining to my situation. If you are in a similar situation, I share them here with you:

God said in Deuteronomy 10:18 that He defends the cause of the fatherless and the widow, and He loves the foreigner residing among you, giving them food and clothing.

Psalm 68:5 calls him a Father to the fatherless, a Defender of widows, and is God in His holy dwelling.

Job 29:12 says because I delivered the poor who cried for help and the orphan who had no helper.

Psalm 10:14 mentions you have been the helper of the orphan.

We are encouraged by Jeremiah 19:11 to leave your orphans behind; I will keep them alive.

Affirmations & Antidotes That Remind Me

Jeremiah 22:3 instructs us to not mistreat or do violence to the stranger, the orphan.

Isaiah 1:17 says to defend the orphan.

Exodus 22:22-24 reads, "You shall not afflict any widow or orphan. If you afflict him at all, and if he does cry out to Me, I will surely hear his cry."

John 14:18 reads, "I will not leave you as orphans; I will come to you. God is the Great Protector and loving Father of all children living as orphans."

Psalm 119:73 states your hands made me and fashioned me; give me understanding, that I may learn your commandments.

Psalm 139:13-14 reminds us, "For you formed my inward parts; you move me in my mother's womb. I will give thanks to you, for I am fearfully and wonderfully made; wonderful are your works, and my soul knows it very well."

In Esther 2:7, Mordecai had a cousin named Hadassah whom he had brought up because she had neither father nor mother. This young woman, who was also known as Esther, had a lovely figure and was beautiful. Mordecai had taken her as his own daughter when her parents died. This story from the Bible keeps my heart at peace, knowing that God took that young girl from being an orphan to becoming a queen. I found comfort in those verses - one of the most powerful stories from the Bible that gave me life daily.

May my story touch your heart to know that no matter what, God will never abandon you. Fix your crown, woman! God got you! Amen!

An Anthology by Dr. Marilyn E. Porter

SHARLRITA DELOATCH

Sharlrita DeLoatch is fearless, relentless, and authentically walking in her God-give purpose. Servant, wife, and mother first, she boldly claims her life as a Speaker, Author, Mentor, and is known as The Life Rebuilding Strategist. Sharlrita is the "Secret Weapon" to Emerging Women Entrepreneurs. She takes women on a journey to Rebuild, Refocus, and Release everything that is in them.

Connect with Sharlrita at:
www.SharlritaSpeaks.com

Affirmations & Antidotes That Remind Me

AFFIRMATIONS:

I AM FEARLESS.
I AM DIVINELY WALKING IN MY PURPOSE.
I LIVE A LIFE OF WEALTH AND BALANCE.
EVERYTHING I TOUCH MULTIPLIES.
I AM NOT THE BEST-KEPT SECRET; I ACKNOWLEDGE WHO I AM AND LET THE WORLD KNOW.
I AM NO LONGER STUCK.
MY PAST NO LONGER HOLDS ME HOSTAGE.
I AM FREE TO BE ME.

REMINDS ME THAT:

These affirmations remind me that no matter what I've done, God can still use me. He can still use a felon, a woman who gave birth out of wedlock, a woman who used to use drugs to teach, speak, and coach women from all over this world.

SHARLRITA'S ANTIDOTE:

With a good pen, paper, a good plan, and a made-up mind, you can and will achieve all that God desires for your life.

An Anthology by Dr. Marilyn E. Porter

MINISTER ALMENA MAYES

Almena L. Mayes is a Licensed Minister who serves as an Associate at Coley Springs Missionary Baptist Church in Warrenton, North Carolina and as Executive Pastor for the Soul Restoration Center in Dallas, Georgia. She also serves as a Facilitator for The Pink Pulpit - a ministry founded and directed by Dr. Marilyn E. Porter.

In 2015, Minister Mayes authored the Best-Selling, semi-autobiographical, inspirational book, Just Eat the Beans, wherein she shares her experiences and knowledge gained through prayer, reflection, and self-esteem building. She holds an Honors Degree in Professional English/Writing from Guilford College in Greensboro, North Carolina.

For information regarding publishing opportunities, public appearances, or speaking engagements, contact Minister Mayes at JustEatTheBeans@gmail.com or on Facebook at Just Eat The Beans.

Affirmations & Antidotes That Remind Me

AFFIRMATION:

I AM UNIQUE AND CUSTOM-DESIGNED FOR A PURPOSE IN GOD'S KINGDOM.

REMINDS ME THAT:

God set a standard when He created each of us. That makes us special. Not only are we the BEST at being who He created us to be; we are the only ones capable of completing our unique assignments! Each of us is God's #1. We are the CEO, the CFO, and the Chairman of the Board in our lives, our purpose, and our promise.

An Anthology by Dr. Marilyn E. Porter

MINISTER MAYES' ANTIDOTE:

"The Lord shall make you the head and not the tail, and you shall be above and you shall not be underneath, if you will listen to the commandments of the Lord your God, which I charge you today, to observe them carefully" (Deuteronomy 28:13).

Self-esteem issues thwart even the best of us. We live in a society where we are constantly bombarded with images that do not reflect reality. Many times, we find ourselves feeling inadequate because we don't meet these perceived standards. Thoughts such as:

"I'm too fat."

"I'm too skinny."

"I'm too light."

"I'm too dark."

"I'm not smart enough."

"I'm not pretty enough."

"I'm incapable of…"

"I just don't measure up to…"

Those thoughts plague our minds, causing us to forget that we are fearfully and wonderfully made!

Being the head and not the tail requires that we have a Kingdom mindset…not a natural one. The Kingdom mindset tells us that when our natural body is riddled with what the world deems as imperfections, we stand perfect in the eyes of God. When the world tells us that we are broke, a Kingdom mindset says there are cattle on a thousand hills that belong to us. We just have to go get them! The world may tell us that we are incapable of being successful, but a Kingdom mindset says that NO weapon formed against us shall prosper.

Affirmations & Antidotes That Remind Me

We are destined to be great because we were created in the image of a Great God!

Being the head and not the tail requires that we forgive ourselves for ever doubting just how phenomenal we truly are. So often, we wallow in our past mistakes - believing they negate our becoming what God promised us. How dare we believe that our opinion of ourselves is more important than that of the One who created us! He sent His only Son that we may be reconciled back to Him and found faultless. He has given us the gift of salvation and His unwavering exoneration.

Being the head and not the tail requires that we act on and by faith. Fear is not a characteristic of those at the top. Faith and fear cannot exist in the same space. Just as light chases away darkness, faith causes fear to flee. There is no way we can claim to know that in God, there is NO failure - and then be afraid to walk boldly wherever God sends us!

Being the head and not the tail requires that we lead! The Father is calling us from among the ordinary to be strange. He desires us to demonstrate a faith walk through difficult situations. We must be the ones who smile in times of distress because we know we will always be victorious. We must be the ones who reassure others that God is with us and always working on our behalf. When the world bows to the whims of the enemy, we are the ones who stand strong and lead the charge against his strongholds.

An Anthology by Dr. Marilyn E. Porter

Finally, as the head and not the tail, we must understand that being the head does not mean we will always be first. Oftentimes, being the head means supporting others in their quests to find what you already have; a definitive image of self that embraces the value God places on us. God's love for us supersedes all expectations. He allows us to experience situations and circumstances that require us to trust His guidance. These may not always be places of comfort. He expects us to extend that same love and guidance to others, even if that means leading them from the rear. Helping others to recognize and move within the realm of God's love is an important part of the work we are called to do.

I have embraced these concepts in my life and found they have brought me to a place of joy and acceptance.

I hope that you, too, can find comfort knowing that no matter what it may look like, you are the head…not the tail.

Affirmations & Antidotes That Remind Me

An Anthology by Dr. Marilyn E. Porter
STEPHANIE STANFORD

Stephanie "Steph" Stanford is an Inspiration-ologist, a Divine Connector, and the Love Empowerment Coach. She helps people connect to the POWER of love. Self-love, Relationship-love, and Life-love contain everything you want and need. She can connect you to new careers, new health, new business, and yes; new people to love. This easy-going chick is a Keynote Speaker, Published Author, and Powerful Coach who has been featured as an expert at The National Black MBA; S Florida Chapter, The University of Miami, numerous conferences, and more than 50 live and online radio shows.

Steph is love in motion! Find out more by visiting: www.StephStanford.com

Affirmations & Antidotes That Remind Me

AFFIRMATION:

I AM ALWAYS RECEIVING GOD'S MESSAGES, SO EVERYTHING IS EASIER. HELP COMES RIGHT TO ME. I AM ABLE TO SEE, HEAR, FEEL, AND KNOW EXACTLY WHAT TO DO AND WHERE TO GO. I AM RECEIVING GOD'S GUIDANCE, SO I CAN RELAX.

REMINDS ME THAT:

I am reminded that it is not "all on me". God's dreams are my dreams. My dreams are God's dreams. So, it's easy to believe that what I need is coming to me. I don't have to stress. I can relax. Ideas, resources, mentors, Divine Helpers, and wisdom are always coming directly to me.

STEPHANIE'S ANTIDOTE:

Surprisingly, my life solution came from my hair. Years ago, when I was at my lowest, I began to read spiritual books. I learned that God is always talking and that we could listen through our bodies. I always hated my hair because it was so out-of-control, so I decided to talk to it…and listen. I told her why I hated her and then I apologized for decades of hate. I thanked her for staying when I didn't love her. She said, "I have overcome chemicals, color, heat, and hate - and I am still here. I am strong. I represent your ancestors who lived hard so you could live easy. You can cut me, fight me, and try to control me, but I am part of God's design…and so are you. We are unstoppable! We will always grow back and win!"

My antidote is this: SLOW DOWN. Make time for quiet. Breathe. Above all, LISTEN. What you hear is not from you: It's God's Divine Help.

An Anthology by Dr. Marilyn E. Porter

STEVII AISHA MILLS

Stevii Aisha Mills is a graduate of North Carolina A&T State University, a strong and ambitious woman whose greatest belief is that when people are given the tools to succeed in life, there is no stopping their potential. With a Bachelor of Arts Degree in Public Relations and a Master's of Science Degree in Human Resources, she is able to align and execute visions, concepts, motivational products, speaking engagements, and workshops for women who are dedicated to pushing past their past and loudly and proudly declaring, "I LOVE MY LIFE!"

Stevii specializes in creating concepts, leadership development, business mentorship, and networking. Her primary goal is empowering women to tap into their God-Give "It Factor". She is an outstanding motivational speaker who connects with her audience through being authentic and showing them they can truly take their lives to their next level of greatness.

When you connect with Stevii, you are guaranteed to have fun, learn, and grow! Visit www.stevii.com

Affirmations & Antidotes That Remind Me

AFFIRMATION:

GOD HAS ALREADY WRITTEN MY BIOGRAPHY. ALL I HAVE TO DO IS CONTINUALLY TURN THE PAGES.

REMINDS ME THAT:

This affirmation reminds me that God has my whole life already planned. He crafted my custom-designed assignment before I was even born.

STEVII'S ANTIDOTE:

No matter what happens - good, bad, ugly, or indifferent - He knows. That blesses me because even in those moments when I just want to give up, I am reminded that I cannot quit and I will not fail because He has already directed the outcome. Even as I write this to you, I am overjoyed because of what God is doing not only in my life, but in your life as well! God cares that much about US! We are, indeed, special and set apart!

An Anthology by Dr. Marilyn E. Porter

TIESHA C. FRONTIS

Tiesha C. Frontis is the Founder and CEO of Know Your Self Worth, Inc. This organization, birthed in 2013, was created to inspire, uplift, and teach women how God sees them and how they should see themselves through Him. She is a native of Charlotte, North Carolina, but relocated to Durham, North Carolina in 1993 to pursue her college education at North Carolina Central University where she graduated with a dual Bachelor Degree in Chemistry and Biology. She is currently pursuing a dual Master's Degree at Pfeiffer College and will also pursue her Doctorate in Theology.

Tiesha is a woman of purpose, faith, and virtue, having persevered through diverse challenges including: molestation, promiscuity, addiction, domestic abuse, miscarriage, homelessness, divorce, and so much more. She lives to share her story with other women and men, encouraging them that they can make it and they can survive.

Affirmations & Antidotes That Remind Me

AFFIRMATION:

I AM CREATED FOR PURPOSE. I AM CREATED IN GOD'S IMAGE TO DOMINATE THE EARTH.

REMINDS ME THAT:

This reminds me that my identity is found in the image of Christ and I have purpose to fulfill because of my creation.

TIESHA'S ANTIDOTE:

"Then God said, "Let us make mankind in our image, in our likeness, so that they may rule over the fish in the sea and the birds in the sky, over the livestock and all the wild animals, and over all the creatures that move along the ground." So, God created mankind in His own image, in the image of God He created them; male and female He created them" (Genesis 1:26-27).

Always remember that God created you to fulfill a purpose in the Earth. It is up to us to find out what that purpose is. When you begin to feel that you have no purpose or feel there is a void in your life, remind yourself and say, "I do have purpose!" "I am created by Christ for a purpose!" "I will complete that which He has ordained just for me to do."

An Anthology by Dr. Marilyn E. Porter

AFFIRMATION:

I AM UNIQUELY CREATED. I AM FEARFULLY AND WONDERFULLY MADE.

REMINDS ME THAT:

This reminds me that I am made with unique characteristics that are specific just to me and how I will fulfill my purpose.

TIESHA'S ANTIDOTE:

"Before I formed you in the womb, I knew you; before you were born, I sanctified you; I ordained you a prophet to the nations" (Jeremiah 1:5).

"I will praise You, for I am fearfully and wonderfully made; marvelous are Your works, and that my soul knows very well" (Psalm 139:14).

"Most assuredly, I say to you, he who believes in Me, the works that I do he will do also; and greater works than these he will do, because I go to My Father" (John 14:12-14).

There may be times in your life when you feel like, "I just don't fit in", "I'm different from everyone else", or (my favorite) "I'm just a loner." Well, to be honest, all of those sayings are correct. You are unique. You are different. You don't fit in with the norm because He set you apart for greatness to do greater works than Him. Remind yourself daily that you are unique in character and cannot be duplicated. Don't be ashamed of who He created you to be. Only you can fulfill the purpose He designed for you to complete. No one else!

Affirmations & Antidotes That Remind Me

AFFIRMATION:

I AM TAKING ON THE IDENITY OF CHRIST.

REMINDS ME THAT:

This reminds me that everything that God made is good and the old becomes new.

TIESHA'S ANTIDOTE:

"For everything God has created is good, and nothing is to be rejected if it is received with gratitude" (1 Timothy 4:4).

"Therefore, if anyone is in Christ, he is a new creation; old things have passed away; behold, all things have become new" (2 Corinthians 5:17).

I find joy in knowing I am not perfect, but I Christ I am perfectly made. Life brings us good and bad; ups and downs; joys and pains; even love and brokenness. The things we need to remember and meditate on both day and night is that with God's grace, we can be made new each and every day. We must know Christ in order to identify with Christ's characteristics. Then we can begin to take on His characteristics so that we can live a life pleasing to Him full of love and peace.

An Anthology by Dr. Marilyn E. Porter

TOYA HAMLETT

A Tennessee native, Toya Hamlett, "#TheVisibilityStrategist", is a repeat #1 Best-Selling Author, Multi History-Making Pageant Queen, Visionary of The Lifestyle of Worship Series, and Community Event Organizer via TDH Unlimited. Some of her services and products include Consulting, Graphics, Print Media, Apparel, and Editing. Toya is a Christian Educator, Choreographer, Public Relations Representative, and serves faithfully in various capacities, locally to international platforms within Sigma Gamma Rho Sorority, Inc., Xcellence, Inc. and the Christian Methodist Episcopal Church, along with other for and non-profits. Ms. Hamlett is an alum of Tennessee State University, with a B.S. in Psychology and Sociology. Her parents are Rev. Terry and Clara Hamlett and she is the sister to Tiffani and Terrica.

For more information, interviews, and/or support, email: toyahamlett3@gmail.com.
Follow her on Instagram/Facebook: toyahamlettwinning
Twitter/Periscope/Snapchat: @ToyaHamlett

Affirmations & Antidotes That Remind Me

AFFIRMATION:

I AM A BEAUTIFUL, WONDERFUL CREATION! FEARFULLY AND WONDERFULLY MADE! TRULY IMPECCABLE BY DESIGN!

REMINDS ME THAT:

This reminds me that I'm innately brilliant! Excellence is ingrained within me.

TOYA'S ANTIDOTE:

"Oh yes, you shaped me first inside, then out; you formed me in my mother's womb. I thank you, High God - you're breathtaking! Body and soul, I am marvelously made! I worship in adoration - what a creation! You know me inside and out, you know every bone in my body; You know exactly how I was made, bit by bit, how I was sculpted from nothing into something. Like an open book, you watched me grow from conception to birth; all the stages of my life were spread out before you, the days of my life all prepared before I'd even lived one day" (Psalm 139:14-16, MSG).

God did not slight me in any way!

"He knows the count of every hair on my head" (Luke 12:7, MSG).

Be innately me! Christ loves me sooo very much! There is still a very specific plan and purpose for my life. I am still here because there are mighty works that are to be performed through ME. In His Word, He said that I would do greater works than He (John 14:12).

An Anthology by Dr. Marilyn E. Porter

"But ye are a chosen generation, a royal priesthood, an holy nation, a peculiar people; that ye should shew forth the praises of Him who hath called you out of darkness into His marvelous light" (1 Peter 2:9).

I am royalty! I am made in His image. When others see me, they see Him. He illuminates through me. I am the righteousness of God. I matter. I am important. My purpose on this Earth is necessary and I must fulfill it. For me, it's spreading the Gospel of Jesus Christ via unique worship experiences across the country and the world. We all have multiple gifts and graces. Embrace them. I also help others become visible in a professional light through the gifts that God has blessed me with. The journey is not predictable - at all. Through prayer, forgiveness, and discernment, we succeed. God shows Himself faithful along the way, via people and encounters.

There is none other like me. I am the only me. I must love me, cherish me, take care of me, and keep me at my best self to fulfill all of what and who I am here for. At times, that includes me distancing myself from others; yet, when I have trouble doing so, and having prayed about it, God will step in and cause the separation. Room has to be made for who and what He has planned for my life.

One of my social media friends, Patrick Weaver, posted, "The Lord says some didn't leave you because they had an issue with you. Some left because they saw your next level and decided leaving was better than slowing you down."

God will work it out! All things work together for my good (Romans 8:28)!

I am innately Brilliant!

Affirmations & Antidotes That Remind Me

An Anthology by Dr. Marilyn E. Porter

ANDRENA PHILLIPS

Andrena Phillips, CEO & Founder of KeepMovinWithAndrena, LLC (KMWA) is a dynamic Master Transformational Life Coach, Motivational Speaker, and Published Author - better known as the ReBuild Life Strategist. KMWA is a movement to spread awareness by helping women become conscious of their purpose and develop life skills that will equip them to live a purposeful life. She is currently using her coaching in workshops and motivational speaking with Dress for Success, Professional Women and other organizational projects locally and worldwide.

Andrena helps women by influencing, empowering, and propelling them to rebuild and develop a blueprint so they can move from struggle to purpose both in their personal and professional goals without apologies.

If you are ready to go to the next level of living, contact Andrena at keepmovinwithandrena@gmail.com for one-on-one coaching, speaking engagements, and interactive workshops.

Affirmations & Antidotes That Remind Me

AFFIRMATION:

MY PURPOSE IS GREATER THAN MY STRUGGLE.

REMINDS ME THAT:

This is my daily affirmation that I breathe, speak, and live. My life's journey has not been easy, but one thing I know: I am equipped for this because I was predestined to succeed.

An Anthology by Dr. Marilyn E. Porter

ANDRENA'S ANTIDOTE:

When you are purposed with a plan, there is no room for losing. You already WON, just because you were created! Purpose has something to do that nobody can get done but you.

See, I am a winner. As soon as I was conceived - before I was named - I was destined for greatness. Being equipped means pushing through when you don't want to and when your back is against the wall - and when those you thought want to see you win actually stab you with their words and actions.

How do you keep getting up when life is demanding, trials and tribulations come and go, and you begin to question why you're here? What are you supposed to do? What does it all mean?

See, you question yourself when you have no clue about your worth and when you allow others to mold you into what they believe you are supposed to be. You find yourself giving your power away to those who don't see your greatness...those who don't want you to see your worth. The moment you gave up is when all the defeated attitudes crept in. The self-pity party started - and you're the only one at the party! The darkness came and it was difficult, but it was the moment you decided whether you want to live or are going to give in.

Affirmations & Antidotes That Remind Me

I choose to LIVE! I realized I didn't conquer everything thrown at me for nothing. I didn't walk through the fire for nothing. I wasn't in the lions' den for me to not come out smelling like "NO Smoke!" I didn't overcome divorce, single motherhood, rejection, low self-esteem, and getting into situations that didn't add up to what I was called to be for nothing. Every step I took…every mountain I climbed…every devil I stomped on will not take my win - the one I had since I was created on July 19th. My life has meaning. Nobody can accomplish the mission GOD created me to do. I realize that it's not the struggle I need to focus on; it's my purpose - that which I was called to do. Nobody can handle what GOD has my name on, so they can't receive the blessings that come with it. I can either accept my greatness that GOD believed so much to put my name on it or I'm telling GOD He wasted His time creating me and that He is a liar.

I searched and searched the Word of GOD trying to see that my life is a waste. Guess what? I can't find a single verse! As a matter-of-fact, I found out I am fearfully and wonderfully made. I'm a King's Kid! I have inheritances I didn't work for and promises that will not come back void. I have no choice but to trust that all this greatness I'm carrying is designed to move mountains. I walk in authority that my name is GREAT!

Many are born, but none can do what I'm called, anointed, and appointed to do. That within itself speaks volumes! ANDRENA'S GOD said she is one-of-a-kind! When you begin to believe and live what GOD says you are, the devil will tremble when he sees you coming because he knows one thing about GOD: Anything GOD created, it can't be beat! Claim your victory! Believe in the GOD in you and never will you question who you are created to be. BE BEAUTIFUL!

An Anthology by Dr. Marilyn E. Porter

YOLANDA CHEATHAM

Yolanda Cheatham wants you to succeed!
As a Life Strategist and Reset Coach, Yolanda inspires and trains women to overcome fear, doubt, and self-limiting beliefs by providing insight, strategic steps, processes, and accountability to transform their mindsets, unleash personal power, and ultimately reach their personal and business goals. Drawing upon her studies of Leading Thought Leaders, professional training in Communications, facilitation, personal development and community relations, her skills are well honed. Yolanda's committed to be an effective catalyst for transformation and results to women across the globe. Guiding her clients through processes to create actionable goals, she also encourages uncovering obstacles and blocks that keep them from moving in forward motion. Yolanda received her B.A. from Clark Atlanta University and Coaching Certificate from The Coaching Institute of Orange County, (ICF approved). As a "post-cancer-thriver," Yolanda knows a little bit about what it takes to reset for intentional living. Her new program, *The Classic Woman's Reset*™, will launch in 2017. In the meantime, she welcomes you to contact her for A Classic Reset Session at info@coachyo.com.

Affirmations & Antidotes That Remind Me

AFFIRMATION:

I AM RESILIENT, BUILT TO LAST, AND EMPOWERED TO OVERCOME ANYTHING. NO WEAPONS FORMED AGAINST ME SHALL PROSPER.

REMINDS ME THAT:

You've probably seen her in your church, at work, or on the 6:00 p.m. news. She's the lady everyone says is strong as nails, unstoppable with resolve and her faith. She went through a tough time but persevered and bounced back. People want to know how she did it. They watch to see if she leaves any clues. She's magnificent, but not magic! She possesses resilience. Perhaps that woman is you...

We are all inspired by such people; remarkable women who seem to reset with intention and soar above the noise and challenges of life. They are moms, wives, entrepreneurs, philanthropists, millionaires, or the woman next door. What makes her different? What does she possess that gives her the ability to make it through setbacks when others lose themselves and fall apart?

The answers don't point to one thing, but rather several qualities, skills, and practices that empower her in times of change and stress. It's called RESILIENCE - a set of skills which can be learned but in others, it is innate, empowering them to manage stress, persevere, and overcome in the face of life's challenges.

An Anthology by Dr. Marilyn E. Porter

Women who overcome adversity are consistently more effective and successful when they have systems and processes to rely on when they are required to make a shift. Simple steps like getting rest and eating healthy can give you bounce-back power when you need it.

YOLANDA'S ANTIDOTE:

Are YOU a resilient woman? How do you react when life shifts unexpectedly? What tools do you have in your tool kit when life tells you to reset? Whether you access these tools in your current challenge or are looking for ways to be more resilient with bounce-back power, here are a few tips you can add to your "Overcomers Tool Kit" to be more brilliantly resilient every day!

- A resilient woman acknowledges her true source of power which empowers her to thrive.
- A resilient woman knows that her commitment to lifelong learning keeps her primed and poised for action and problem-solving that informs her solutions to challenges.
- A resilient woman is flexible and adaptable to change. She is not easily thrown by that which she can't control, and knows how to go with the flow.
- A resilient woman has a sense of humor; she doesn't take life too seriously. She knows that laughter can raise her vibration and elevate her mood.
- A resilient woman listens to her body. Physical resilience depends on her engaging in healthy lifestyle practices. Her body is her temple; her health is her best asset.

Affirmations & Antidotes That Remind Me

- A resilient woman lives in integrity. She embraces her strengths as well as her limitations. She understands that she is human and sometimes, things just don't work out. While failure is not a goal, she perceives setbacks as a lesson learned. She doesn't allow circumstances to define her, and is at peace with the truth - which empowers her to ask for support when needed.

An Anthology by Dr. Marilyn E. Porter

ONIKA SHIRLEY

Onika Shirley is the Founder/CEO of Action Speaks Volume, Inc.™ She is a Global Confidence-Procrastination Coach, Speaker, and Author who helps women build confidence and stop procrastination. As an Action Coach, Onika gives her clients actionable steps to get them thinking positively and change their overall mindset.

Affirmations & Antidotes That Remind Me

AFFIRMATIONS:
ACTION-TAKERS WALK BY FAITH.

I am an action-taker, walking by faith.
I will reap a harvest in due season and faint not.
I will take action to live my dream.
All of my actions will support my vision.
My vision is in the will of God.
I will take concrete steps to actualize my vision.
I will walk by faith and not by sight.
Every day, I will take positive actions directed by God.
I am obedient to the Word of God.
I will accelerate my progress.
When I walk by faith in God, I will increase my motivation.
I am willing to take action.
I am ready to move forward in my life.
I will direct my energy towards positive actions.
I will take charge and take the necessary actions to get things done.
I will start my projects right away.
I will be proactive all the time.
I will not procrastinate.
I will embrace action.
The word "reactive" is not in my vocabulary.
I will not make excuses.
I am unstoppable, unmovable, and unbreakable.
I will take action by faith in spite of my fear.
I will hold myself accountable.

ONIKA'S ANTIDOTE:

Procrastination and Unbelief are the problems.
Faith and Actions are the antidotes.

An Anthology by Dr. Marilyn E. Porter

FELICIA LUCAS

Felicia Lucas is a Minister, #1 International Best-Selling Author, Inspirational Speaker, Empowerment Coach, and Event Planner. She and her husband, Pastor Kelvin Lucas, Co-Founded *Take It By Force Ministries, Inc.*, a non-profit 501(c)3 organization, and *Dominion Tabernacle Church*. They were married in 1997 and have three children. As a business woman on the move, Felicia is the CEO of *His Glory Creations* and *A Moment in Time*. She graduated from the University of North Carolina at Chapel Hill. For over 20 years, she has worked in the Human Resources field.

Additional information can be found by visiting www.felicialucas.com.

Affirmations & Antidotes That Remind Me

AFFIRMATION:

JUST BECAUSE WE DON'T SEE GOD DOESN'T MEAN WE DON'T SEE GOD!

REMINDS ME THAT:

This reminds me that even though we don't physically see God with our natural eyes, we can see the evidence of His works all around us.

An Anthology by Dr. Marilyn E. Porter

FELICIA'S ANTIDOTE:

About two weeks before I was scheduled to return from my maternity leave for my last child, I received a phone call that stated I needed to be on a conference call for work. I was working as a Human Resources Manager for a national retail company. I went ahead and signed on to the call. Having no idea what the call was about, I sat nervously and anxiously waiting for the information. I was informed the company was going through a reorganization and, as a result, 2,200 associates were going to be laid off - which included me.

I returned to work for my remaining weeks. I remember my assistant saying to me, "Oh, Felicia: You just had a baby! What are you going to do?" Without hesitation, I said, "TRUST GOD!" Surprisingly, I did not become stressed or angry about the situation. I didn't even cry. I had faith to believe that God had my back and He would provide. Looking back, I am amazed I had that level of faith!

A few weeks later, I received a phone call for an interview from a company I don't even remember applying to. After the interview, they called me back and offered me a job which paid more than my laid-off job, provided more life balance, and more growth opportunities. God turned what could have been a bad situation and provided provision.

Prior to the layoff, God showed His ability to provide. My husband and I are Co-Founders of a non-profit 501(c)3 youth and young adult organization. We primarily rely on donations as our source of income for events. There are two specific times when we were short in making our financial budget. One month, before one of the events, we received an invitation to facilitate a week-long youth Summer Camp at a local church. The organizers of the event asked what our fee was to do the camp, and we said, "Whatever you give us is fine!"

Affirmations & Antidotes That Remind Me

The amount they paid us was the exact amount of our deficit. After receiving the check, I asked them, "Why that amount?" They said, "That was the amount God told us to pay!"

My next incident is very similar to the first, but the amount needed was greater. I heard on our local Christian radio station about a promotion where they would be giving out a cash prize for a contest. All the listener had to do was review an advertisement in the Sunday circular and be prepared to answer questions concerning it. The next day, the radio DJ announced the contest and that caller #1 would win the money if they provided the correct answer. With a fast-beating heart, I dialed the number. Guess who caller #1 was? I won the $1,000.00 cash prize! We met the budget and the event was successful!

Thank you, God, for your faithfulness!

An Anthology by Dr. Marilyn E. Porter

NOTES TO SELF

Affirmations & Antidotes That Remind Me

An Anthology by Dr. Marilyn E. Porter

Affirmations & Antidotes That Remind Me

An Anthology by Dr. Marilyn E. Porter

Affirmations & Antidotes That Remind Me

An Anthology by Dr. Marilyn E. Porter

Affirmations & Antidotes That Remind Me

An Anthology by Dr. Marilyn E. Porter

Affirmations & Antidotes That Remind Me

An Anthology by Dr. Marilyn E. Porter

Affirmations & Antidotes That Remind Me

An Anthology by Dr. Marilyn E. Porter

Affirmations & Antidotes That Remind Me

An Anthology by Dr. Marilyn E. Porter

Affirmations & Antidotes That Remind Me

An Anthology by Dr. Marilyn E. Porter

CONTACT DR. MARILYN E. PORTER

FOR BOOKINGS, CONTACT
DR. PORTER VIA EMAIL :
INFO@MARILYNEPORTER.COM

OTHER M.E. PORTER TITLES

IF YOU ENOYED THIS BOOK,
HERE ARE OTHER M.E. PORTER TITLES:

The Pieces of ME (And YOU)

HERstory Reveals His Glory

Though I Walk (Divine Healing in The Valley)

COMING IN 2017

Motivation for Mompreneurs (May)

Stories from The Pink Pulpit (June)

By The Still Waters (July)

Affirmations That Heal ME (September)

www.ingramcontent.com/pod-product-compliance
Lightning Source LLC
Chambersburg PA
CBHW071745080526
44588CB00013B/2159